SISTERS IN SHAME

by
johnny solstice

Published by
Iliffe Independent
Leeds, UK

ISBN 978-1-909110-06-9

www.iliffe.org.uk

is your
competitor
on the conveyor
belt
chastity belt
lottery bet
lovelier yet
beauty never
sets

soul sister
raise a blister
on this system
that binds you
and blinds you
where your
sister

onwards
upwards
higher heights
pure delights
late at night

Her timing was
her function
She felt it in her
junction
box clever
soul sister
flowing ever

never can reject

your essence
your presence
don't need
presents

or pasts
just futures
your features
are your teacher
beware of preachers
avoid creatures
selling potions
and lotions
to improve your
perception
of who you are

Hey mister!
You missed her
My sister
Religious twisters
Have twisted their
minds
Against all womankind

Pouring
chemicals
through her vein
Programming
her that she has
no brain
Breaking her
feet with
bondage shoes

Poisoning her
skin with
pigments and
hues

Don't get
confused

By marketing men
Dealing in yearn
And making you earn
More than you need
Spike you with greed
Give you sterile seeds
For barren soil
And sell you oil
For your hair

Make you stare
In disbelief
At someone else

Who isn't you
Hasn't a clue
What constitutes you-
So
be bold
be noble

forget that dress

REHEARSAL-
UNIVERSAL
ADDIKTION-
GENDER
FRIKTION-

COMPLEKTION
IMPERFEKTION

Don't lissen sista-
To anyone called
"missed her"-
Not assister-
But a hamper-
Put a damper-
On your ambition-
Use a partition-
Of suppression-
Of your divinity-

Your connection to the
mother-
Makes your brother-
Just another-
Distraction-
Attraction-
Contraction-
Chemikal reaction-

Remember?-

Pang of guilt?-

Don't quit-

The freedom is worth it-
So! No, don't quit-
Learn to hit-
Back-
At lack-
Of respect-
And learn to rejekt-

Suspect advances-
Learn old dances-
Whilst patriarchy
prances-
Adopt stances-
More positive to
branches-
Of learnin-
And yearning
for pleasure-

Discover your treasure-
Without measure-
Try passion
flowers-
By the hour-
By the minute
-By the moment-

Watch for
homing instinct
Don't become
extinct-
In search of a
thrill-
t aint in a pill
Or a potion-
Try this notion

You are divine-
You can't be mine-
Coz property's a crime-
Against humanity-
Avoid adversity-
And perversity-
Don't become a kitchen
accessory-
Don't be a bedroom
necessity-
Don't be someone else's
fantasy-

Be who YOU
wanna be-
Be free-
Of pressure-
Don't measure –
Your body-

Don't compete-
Don't deplete-
You are complete-
You are unique-
Run from conceit-
Walk down your street-
With a smile in your step-
And your shoulders back-
Wear your clothes slack
Get the fashion munkey
off your back-
All that you lack-
Is nothing at all-
Walk tall-
You are woman-After all-
Go to the ball-

Don't wear glass
slippers-
Avoid jealous sisters-
Don't get blisters-
From working out-
Or working in-
Domestik slavery-
You need a medal for
bravery-
To live in this century-
Of so called liberation-

Where
permission is
granted-
To sink to their
level-
Of equality-

Be who you wanna be-
Be free-
Be she
-Don't lissen to he-
Except when you wanna
be-
What you wanna be-
Just be-
What you wamma be-
Be she-
Be free-

See your destiny-
There's more to this than
a hand on your knee-
And flattery-
And femininty-
And perversity-
Of purpose!-
Get out of the circus-
Don't perform for ring-
masters-
Take off your ring
Let them bring-
The world to **your** feet-

Know yourself-
Let no one judge you-
Or measure you-
Or treasure you-
Like they discovered
you
-Like you were lost and
they found you-
And impound you
On a pedestal-

Yeah don't let vanity-
affect your sanity-
don't lissen to profanity-
directed at your body-
by someone who's
agenda is different from
yours-

don't buy cures-
for aging-
or slimming-
remember winning-
aint living-
you are timeless-
you are ageless-
you are mother-
you are no other-
but sister-to the world-

don't let them pierce
you-
or cut you-
or starve you
into being someone you
are not-
somehow they forgot-
how to see your beauty-
they judge you in a
swimsuit-
they judge your very
skin-

everyone's unhappy
even when they're thin-

most peoples problem?
they're not someone else
In this climate of
dissatisfaction-
Counting fractions-
Of ounces-
fighting nature-
Fighting yourself-

Wearing one size
smaller-
Wearing shoes to be
taller-
Sell your breasts for a
dollar-

And dance if
your able-
On top of a
table-

So you're able-
To feed your
baby-
And later
maybe-
Go university-

Study perversity
Of purpose-

Buy a rose
Buy a razor-
Eyebrow erasor-
Chemikal shaver-
Paint your face-
Spray your body with
U.V. mace-
Join the race-

To the alter-
Don't falter-

Eyes on the prize-
Measure your thighs-
Don't be a prize-
In anyone's game-
Don't live with the
shame-
Of being to blame
For your name-
That came-
From your father-

Not your mother-
Or any other-
Know yourself-
Find yourself-
Be yourself-
Discover yourself-
Uncover yourself-
Love yourself-
For who you are

No man with a car-
Or a big cigar-
Can put you in a jar-
Or wear you on his arm
-Like a specimen-
Acquisition-
To enhance his position-
Of being no-one
important-
To the rules of the
game-

It's all the same-
They teach you shame-
Then offer you fame-
Or a job on the board-
And you think you've
scored-
But it's just an own-goal
Coz jobs with the boys-
And your very own toys
Are just ploys-

To get you to play-
In their games-
Adopt their names
Play power-games-
In the playground-
With violence-
And silence-
That ends where??-

Where it began-
Woman and man-
Adam and Eve-
Would you believe-
A bite of an apple-
Guess who's to blame-
Yeah the games the
same-
Sisters in shame-

A bite of an apple-
Sisters in shame-
Original sin –
Sisters in shame-
Pile on the guilt-
Spill the milk-
That they suck from
your breast-
While they build you a
nest-

And offer you
beads-
And ignore your
needs-
And train you to
breed-
And fail to
succeed-

Till you have a
need-
To rely on
THEM-

Yeah them-
You know
them?-

Who need to con-trol
someone else-
Someone smaller
-Someone weaker-
Someone less able-
Than their impotent
lives

-Searching for wives-
To be obedient-
To show to their mates
That they've got what it takes-
To keep you in your place

And a pedestal is as much a prison as any small confined space

Yes a pedestal is as much a prison as any small confined space